CW01064981

# FIRST JOHN

## CHRISTIANITY IN THE SECOND AND TWENTY FIRST CENTURIES

PIETER VAN STADEN

© 2021 by PWJ van Staden.

All rights reserved.

The scripture quotations are taken from the NIVUK: Holy Bible, New International Version® Anglicized, NIV® Copyright © 1979, 1984, 2011 by Biblica, Inc.® Used by permission. All rights reserved worldwide.

Cover design by Danie van Straaten

ISBN: 9798513967200

# TABLE OF CONTENTS

# INDEX

# Overview

One of the oldest questions in Philosophy has to do with how undeniable knowledge can be obtained. This issue has become very important for Christians in the information age. The early Christian church was plagued by false doctrines propagated by the so-called gnostics. They claimed to have personal knowledge of the divine.

Paul opposed these heresies in several of his letters. The first epistle of John was written decades after the death of Paul. Flawed theology was still plaguing the church. Since that time until today people are being led astray by false teaching. John did not beat about the bush in addressing it.

One can be forgiven for being confused about Christians, Christ followers, the Emerging Church, Progressive Christianity and other phrases and buzzwords used to describe those who identify with the label "Christian". John Stott identified in the first epistle of John certain tests which one can apply to decide if a person is a true follower of Jesus. He grouped the tests into three main categories:

1. Moral – keeping God's commands;
2. Social – loving one another;
3. Doctrinal – believing Jesus is the Jewish Messiah and Son of God.

There are other Bible passages which back up the claim that God expects his people to have those three traits. Paul wrote that faith, hope and love will remain even after knowledge passes away (1 Corinthians 13:13). According

# INTRODUCTION

to John we overcome the world by our faith (1 John 5:4). He links our hope to having good morals (1 John 3:3) and love is at the heart of his letters. Those who are "of the devil" are marked by their evil deeds and lack of love. Liars and antichrists deny that God became a human being in the person of Jesus Christ.

John wrote his first letter to encourage Jesus followers that they could know they had eternal life. The letter can still help its readers to answer the questions: "Do I believe in Jesus? Do I keep God's commands? Do I love other believers?" If the answer to any of the questions is "No", the reader has reason to question his/her salvation.

The letter also serves the purpose of recognising false teachers. Those who teach others are judged more strictly (James 3:1). Every believer must ask the question: "Whom do I listen to? Are they walking like Jesus walked?" In a world where information is available at the touch of a screen these questions are of the utmost importance.

In the post-modern world unhealthy relationships among family members have become common. Jesus predicted that it would happen (Matthew 10:21 & Luke 21:16). Biblical marriage is not the norm in our society. Self-centredness is not regarded as a bad trait in Hollywood culture. Paul prophesied that that would be typical of the last days (2 Timothy 3:2). But common sense tells us that any two or more self-absorbed people are unlikely to get along well. A person who must always have his/her own way is likely to end up alone. In some cities of Europe more than half the population live in a household of one person.

The gap which arises because of the absence of flesh and blood company is mostly filled by phones and screens. These can be switched on or off so that one's independence is assured. The lack of intimacy is often made up by voyeurism because the human soul longs for companionship. This pastime creates unrealistic expectations which further erode relationships.

Many influential leaders of our day are propagating the acceptance of values which mirror our broken society. They regard morality as relative to the occasion and the people involved. Absolute values and objective truth are not acceptable to someone who is used to making his/her own rules.

To understand the Western culture of the 21$^{st}$ century it is instructive to explore how it evolved. The Judeo-Christian ethic prevailed in Europe for the best part of the period beginning in 313AD (Constantine's Edict of Milan) until the so-called "Age of Enlightenment" of the 17$^{th}$ and 18$^{th}$ centuries. The influence of the Roman Catholic Church on the Holy Roman Empire was eroded by the Protestant Reformation of the 16$^{th}$ century and later by the French Revolution of 1787-1799. The last Holy Roman Emperor abdicated his title two years after Napoleon had crowned himself the Emperor of France in 1804.

By the year 1900AD "enlightened thinking" had become the dominant motivating force in Western culture. During the 19$^{th}$ and 20$^{th}$ centuries academics in the humanities were influenced by the success of the natural sciences in advancing technology. Applying the "scientific method" to Psychology, Sociology and even Theology became the norm. The theory of evolution gained acceptance among educators of all disciplines.

The phrase "Scientia est lux lucis", which is Latin for 'knowledge is light of light', is attributed to Leonardo da Vinci (1452 – 1519). Today's popular culture accepts as fact those ideas which can be "scientifically proven". Everything else is regarded as speculation. Sin and salvation are not recognised as objective realities. This is in stark contrast to statements made in John's three short pastoral letters. In them he uses two Greek words, both of which indicate knowledge and certainty, 40 times.

We know objectively that our sins are forgiven and we have eternal life because of the witness of John and the thousands of Christians who lived before us. Subjectively we have the witness of the Holy Spirit and have come to know the Father and the Son. We are in a relationship with our Creator and accountable to him. Power over sin or sickness is not attainable by secret knowledge as the gnostics claimed.

Against the pressure to compromise their values John urged his readers to love one another. It is not our mission to bash other Christians (James 3:19-21). If they confess Jesus they are on our side (Luke 9:49-50). He warns his readers against idolatry, that is loving the pleasure, pretty things and prestige of this world. Idolatry will damage one's faith and make one insensitive to those in need (Ezekiel 16:49-50).

# Preface

In this brief commentary I have attempted to indicate the relevance of John's letter to Christians today. The works of Francis Schaeffer have been helpful. I have also made use of information obtainable on the internet as well as three older commentaries:

The Letters of John and Jude by William Barclay (1958);

The Epistles of John by John Stott (1964);

The Message of John's Letters by David Jackman (1988).

My approach was to use the text to address modern day ideologies which are similar to the ones the early church contended with. Among those who can benefit greatly from this work are students who are exposed to theories relating to purpose, meaning and ethics. A characteristic of many universities in the 21$^{st}$ century is the intolerance their academics and management have of dissenting views. My style is both devotional and confrontational. The intention is for seekers of truth to expand their knowledge of the controversial issues raised and to gain confidence in their faith.

To obtain maximum benefit from this work I strongly recommend the reader to take note of how the commentary addresses the text of the epistle. An equally important suggestion is having a search engine handy to look up the meaning of some words and to read wider on the historic references. Finally, many of the statements are backed up by Bible references, given in parentheses. It is therefore highly desirable to read this book with a Bible at hand.

# 1. Friendship with Jesus (1:1-4)

**1** That which was from the beginning, which we have heard, which we have seen with our eyes, which we have looked at and our hands have touched—this we proclaim concerning the Word of life. 2 The life appeared; we have seen it and testify to it, and we proclaim to you the eternal life, which was with the Father and has appeared to us. 3 We proclaim to you what we have seen and heard, so that you also may have fellowship with us. And our fellowship is with the Father and with his Son, Jesus Christ. 4 We write this to make our[a] joy complete. {[a] some versions say your joy}

Epistemology is the branch of Philosophy which has to do with how we know anything. When Pilate asked Jesus: "What is truth" (John 18:37-38), he probably did not expect an answer.

René Descartes (1596-1650) set himself the task of reinventing philosophy. He would base all theories on some fact of which everyone could have absolute certainty. The only such fact he could come up with was "I think therefore I am". Blaise Pascal (1623-1662) was highly critical of Descartes's view of the world and wrote: "I cannot forgive Descartes. In all his philosophy he would have been quite willing to do without God. But he had to make Him flick a finger to set the world in motion; beyond this, he has no further need of God."

John the apostle, on the other hand, claimed to know that Jesus was divine. He used the word "know" over and over in this letter, confident that he was not mistaken. He was confident enough to dedicate his whole life to propagating what Jesus had called "the Good News"; he was convinced that the rabbi he had followed was none other than the Son of God. The Jesus in whose company he travelled, ate, drank and slept had existed "from the beginning". Here, as in John 1:1, he was clearly alluding to Genesis 1:1. The man Jesus was the "Word of God" who appeared to the prophets mentioned in the Old Testament.

John's fellow apostle Peter was in full agreement with that sentiment. They were not passing on clever myths; they were eyewitnesses of Jesus' majesty (2 Peter 1:16). Paul also emphasised the fact that the Son existed before anything in creation (Colossians 1:16-17). He had "emptied himself" to become a man (Philippians 2:6-8).

John used the phrase "Word of life" to refer both to Jesus and to the message of eternal life as proclaimed by the apostles. Jesus had told them to preach the good news. It goes beyond human philosophy. It is life-giving, capable of bringing about new birth resulting in a relationship with our Creator (1 Peter 1:23). Our ancestors Adam and Eve were banished from Eden after they had lost their close connection with God. John witnessed God living in the form of a human being and inviting him, his brother and their friends into his presence.

One of John's aims with the letter was to invite his readers into friendship with Jesus and his Father and also friendship with himself and other followers of Jesus. To describe such a relationship he uses a phrase similar to the one he had heard from Jesus on his way to Gethsemane. Joy is the hallmark of believers who keep Jesus' commandments (John 15:10-12).

# 2. Light and darkness (1:5-7)

5 This is the message we have heard from him and declare to you: God is light; in him there is no darkness at all. 6 If we claim to have fellowship with him and yet walk in the darkness, we lie and do not live out the truth. 7 But if we walk in the light, as he is in the light, we have fellowship with one another, and the blood of Jesus, his Son, purifies us from all[b] sin. {[b] some versions say every sin}

After John had made the case of why he should be viewed a trustworthy witness, and announced his purpose for writing, he proceeded to the essence of what he wanted to bring across to his readers: Light and darkness which can be described in terms of good and evil, truth and falsehood or love and hate.

After Adam and Eve had sinned they avoided the presence of God; shame caused them to hide themselves. Sin broke Adam's relationship with God. He became separated from God. Then he separated himself from his wife and blamed her for his sin. Eve blamed the snake. The devil's agenda to this day is still to draw people away from their Creator.

In the 21st century one of the most potent weapons of satan is the lure of pornography. Millions are dabbling in it and as a result live with shame. John calls that "walking in darkness". A modern saying would be "living a lie". If we claim to be close to God or enjoy his approval while hiding our deeds behind an attitude of self-righteousness we are lying. Directly translated from the Greek, we are "not doing the truth".

A person with a lifestyle filled with shameful secrets is bound to have difficulty in relating to others. Brené Brown (https://brenebrown.com) has done extensive research on the effect shame has on our behaviour. Shaming someone or experiencing shame erodes trust. If any good could come from such behaviour, it would be in getting us to seek forgiveness from God and those we have hurt.

Paul wrote that the devil makes himself to look like an angel of light (2 Corinthians 11:14). In the Latin version of the Bible Isaiah 14:12 uses the word lucifer for the king of Babylon. Many commentators believe this refers to satan. The word means "light-bearer". In the King James Bible this was turned into a proper noun, giving satan a name. Jesus did not afford him that honour. In Revelation 12:9 he is called "the great dragon that ancient serpent called the devil, or satan".

We can live with clear consciences in spite of the fact that we still have sinful desires and attitudes because the blood of Jesus cleanses us from all sin. This will be the case provided our lives can be described by: "what you see is what you get". Notice that "purifies" in verse 7 is present tense. Light is not directly observed; we see the true nature of an object when light shines on it (Psalm 36:9). When people are in the light they can see and be seen by each other. The outcome of a transparent lifestyle is "fellowship with one another". Here John refers to our association with other believers.

According to the Westminster Shorter Catechism "The chief end of man is to glorify God and enjoy Him forever."

# 3. Honest to God (1:8-9)

8 If we claim to be without sin, we deceive ourselves and the truth is not in us. 9 If we confess our sins, he is faithful and just and will forgive us our sins and purify us from all unrighteousness.

The idea that humans are good by nature is one of the most damaging lies propagated at institutes of higher learning. It is alleged that people are born good but become bad because of the pain they experienced, or the damage done to them while they were children. They deny that we have a sinful nature. Rather, exposure to harmful influences supposedly cause us to become "anti-social". This belief is in direct contradiction with the teaching of Jesus. He called all to repentance (Mark 1:15). If we insist that we are without sin we delude ourselves and are devoid of the truth (Romans 3:23).

Science has brought incredible innovation and improvement to our lives. The scientific method is based on experiments which can be repeated. Physics and Chemistry are examples of disciplines belonging to this class. Also, great advances in medicine have been achieved through studies in Anatomy and Physiology. Ken Ham correctly labels the theory of evolution as "historical science" in contrast to "observational science". It is not possible to conduct an experiment in which the earth would be recreated. Neither has anyone been successful in creating the simplest living organism (https://inference-review.com/article/time-out).

The Darwinian principle of continuity requires faith since it cannot be verified by repeatable experiments. There have been attempts to formulate the foundations of Mathematics on pure logic without accepting any axioms. Kurt Gödel demonstrated this to be impossible, compelling even mathematicians to make assumptions by faith.

The theory of evolution has not contributed to any of the technological advances which improved society. However, it has had a major impact on the social sciences. Richard Weikart published the book From Darwin to Hitler. The title says it all. Hitler believed the human race would be improved if weaker races were eliminated. He regarded the Jews as such a race. One may say he wanted to speed up the process of Darwinian natural selection in which only the fittest survive.

Contrary to the modern consensus Moses wrote more than three thousand years ago: "In the beginning God created the heavens and the earth" (Genesis 1:1). The prophet Jeremiah exclaimed: "The heart is deceitful above all things and beyond cure. Who can understand it?" (Jeremiah 17:9). It follows that we did not descend from apelike creatures. God would be unjust to accuse such a creature of wrongdoing. John was saying the same thing when he wrote that we would be deceiving ourselves if we denied the sinful nature we inherited from Adam.

It is not possible for any of us to undo the sins we have committed. We have to be forgiven by God. He promised to forgive us if we confess them and believe that Jesus paid with his life to restore our relationship with the Father. God forgives us for Christ's sake; he is not about to ignore the price his Son paid to redeem us from from the grip sin had on us (John 8:34; Romans 6:6). God's faithfulness compels him to be true to his promises.

# 4. The remedy for sin (1:10-2:2)

10 If we claim we have not sinned, we make him out to be a liar and his word is not in us.

2 My dear children, I write this to you so that you will not sin. But if anybody does sin, we have an advocate with the Father —Jesus Christ, the Righteous One. 2 He is the atoning sacrifice for our sins, and not only for ours but also for the sins of the whole world.

By "walking in the light" John was not suggesting that we can reach a stage of sinless perfection. To claim that we don't need forgiveness is tantamount to calling God a liar. If we had his word in us we would know that we were not sin free. If his word forbids something, he will not accept an excuse such as "I didn't hurt anyone". As we grow closer to God we are likely to become more aware of our sinful nature rather than to think "we have arrived".

Jesus did not teach that only some believers were "saints". He rejected the idea that one could obtain higher levels of Christianity by working one's way up (Luke 18:9-14). He did not encourage his followers to give their leaders titles (Matthew 23:8-11). In Revelation 11:18 it is written that Jesus will reward all those who fear God's name, both small and great. Not all believers receive the same reward (Luke 19:12-24).

The fact that everybody sins does not mean that we should relax in our attitude to sin. We must never forget what it cost God to save us. When Adam and Eve sinned, God promised that a man would come who would crush the devil's head. That man is now our advocate.

It is wrong to think that since Jesus acts as our advocate, he therefore needs to save us from God. Through our sins we harm ourselves as well as those we sin against. We need help to resist the temptations that come our way. The Father sent Jesus to save us from the grip of sin. Sin is what separates us from the Almighty. One of the most well-known verses in the Bible contains the phrase "God so loved the world" (John 3:16). It is reasonable that the anger of God should remain on those who reject his only Son (John 3:36).

After sinning Adam and Eve felt shame because of their nakedness. The Lord covered them with clothes of skin. An animal had to die (Genesis 3:15, 21). Whenever God forgives sin he does it on these terms. All the godly people like Abel, Noah, Job, Abraham and many more, sacrificed animals when they worshipped. Sins are forgiven when a blood sacrifice has been be offered and the sinner covered. (The Hebrew word for "cover" is "kippur" which is often translated "atonement". In Hebrew the Day of Atonement is Yom Kippur.)

In the covenant God made with the Israelites at Sinai he made provision for a high priest as a mediator between the people and God. The high priest would offer sacrifices on behalf of himself and also for the people. In the new covenant Jesus is the only person who can fulfil this role (John 14:6; Hebrews 4:15). He is also the sacrifice himself who gave his life as a ransom for many (Mark 10:45; Hebrews 9:12). He will represent anyone in the world who so wishes (Acts 2:21). Those who make use of his invitation he covers with his righteousness (2 Corinthians 5:21).

# 5 Reality check (2:3-6)

3 We know that we have come to know him if we keep his commands. 4 Whoever says, "I know him," but does not do what he commands is a liar, and the truth is not in that person. 5 But if anyone obeys his word, love for God[a] is truly made complete in them. This is how we know we are in him: 6 Whoever claims to live in him must live as Jesus did.
{[a] or God's love}

We can be assured that we have come to know God if we take his commands seriously (John 14:15).

In this passage John does not use the term "we" when he refers to wrongdoing. He asserts that anyone ("whoever") who claims to know God, but who disregards his commands is a liar. Jesus insisted that a person's character can be judged from his/her actions, just like a tree is known by its fruit (Matthew 7:15-16).

George Verwer (founder of Operation Mobilization) wrote a book entitled Pseudo-discipleship. A pseudo-disciple is someone who supposedly follows Christ, but does so with sinful motivations, methods or attitudes. We live in a day when shameless sin is not only tolerated but encouraged in some churches.

In his book The Cost of Discipleship Dietrich Bonhoeffer claims that "Cheap grace is grace without discipleship, grace without the cross, grace without Jesus Christ, living and incarnate".

Every method God has ever used to reach man, man has managed to pervert. This happens because in everyone of us the sinful nature shouts: "I'll do it my way". When God required blood sacrifices the practice degenerated into child sacrifices. The commandments given to Israel were externalised by teachers of the Law. Jesus uttered his harshest rebukes to the hypocrites who claimed to keep the Law. They were so blinded by their self-righteousness that they would tithe on everything they earned but they neglected to show kindness (Matthew 23: 23). No wonder that they did not recognise the Giver of the Law when he appeared in the flesh.

Jesus spoke to the crowds in parables because he did not want them to turn the salvation he offered into another formula (Luke 8:10). This is exactly what has happened to Luther's declaration: "sola fide". By that he proclaimed that a person is made right with God by "faith alone". Some church members who have been christened as infants are told that they are saved by "grace alone" and many of them have no idea of what it means to be a follower of Jesus.

Today there are those who put their faith in the knowledge that they have made a decision to accept Jesus as Saviour or that they have been baptised. But their speech and their actions betray their true nature (James 2:18). We will remain in his love if we obey him just as he obeyed his Father (John 15:10). It is not what we know that makes us believers but Whom we know.

Another quote by Dietrich Bonhoeffer reads: "Being a Christian is less about cautiously avoiding sin than about courageously and actively doing God's will."

# 6. A new commandment (2:7-11)

7 Dear friends, I am not writing you a new command but an old one, which you have had since the beginning. This old command is the message you have heard. 8 Yet I am writing you a new command; its truth is seen in him and in you, because the darkness is passing and the true light is already shining. 9 Anyone who claims to be in the light but hates a brother or sister[b] is still in the darkness. 10 Anyone who loves their brother and sister[c] lives in the light, and there is nothing in them to make them stumble. 11 But anyone who hates a brother or sister is in the darkness and walks around in the darkness. They do not know where they are going, because the darkness has blinded them.

{[b]&[c] Greek adelphos can be masculine or feminine}

Jesus said his disciples would be known by their love for one another (John 13:35). Although he called it a new commandment, Jesus had always asserted that love for God and "neighbour" was the heart of the Law and the Prophets (Matthew 22:40). Other experts of the Jewish Bible agreed with this (Mark 12:28-34; Luke 10:25-28).

The "new" commandment is true, not just because it makes sense intellectually, but it is experienced. The first sign of being enlightened is a new love for others of the same persuasion. By copying the incredible love Jesus demonstrated for his friends, those who live in loving relationships with fellow believers experience the true meaning of the Law of Moses.

When Jesus came into the world he brought light. It is not possible for someone who embraces the light to hate one of his brothers or sisters. A person consumed by hatred will be confused. If I am hurt by someone and don't forgive I will become obsessed with that person and lose my focus. This is the case with some who are divorced. Holding a grudge causes one to lose perspective and have a twisted view of reality. Those who claim to have come to the light but don't act the part are still in the dark.

There are several accounts in the Bible about the hatred real blood brothers had for each other. The first man born of a woman murdered his brother (Genesis 4:8). Jacob feared for his life because of his twin (Genesis 27:41). Jacob's sons came very close to killing their brother. Instead, they sold him into slavery (Genesis 37:18, 28).

David's brothers did not treat him kindly when he went to bring them food at the battle front (1 Samuel 17:28). But his greatest heartache must have been the toxic relationships among his own sons. Absalom murdered Amnon for raping his sister (2 Samuel 13:28). Even Solomon put one of his brothers to death because he had made a grab for the throne (1 Kings 1:5; 2:25).

In Psalm 133 David said "brothers dwelling together in unity" are like "the precious oil ... upon ... Aaron's beard". How did he arrive at this unusual comparison of brothers, oil and beard? Was he reflecting on the way Moses and his brother Aaron got along? Moses had anointed him with oil and they served God together for 40 years, even though their relationship had also gone through an unhealthy patch (Numbers 12:1).

# 7. You can do it (2:12-14)

12    I am writing to you, dear children, because your
      sins have been forgiven on account of his name.
13    I am writing to you, fathers, because you
      know him who is from the beginning.
      I am writing to you, young men, because
      you have overcome the evil one.
14    I write to you, dear children, because
      you know the Father.
      I write to you, fathers, because
      you know him who is from the beginning.
      I write to you, young men,
      because you are strong,
      and the word of God lives in you,
      and you have overcome the evil one.

The letters (epistles) of the New Testament begin with an introduction in which the author identified himself and the intended recipients – that is, all the letters except for 1 John and the letter to the Hebrews. John only addressed his readers in 2:2. He used the word "teknia", a diminutive or term of endearment. It is usually translated "little children" or "dear children". In 2:7 he uses the word "agapetio" which is best translated "beloved" rather than "dear friends" as in the NIV.

Commentators like William Barclay and John Stott have speculated about the meaning of the above verses. One fact to take into account when interpreting them is that the term John used seven times in this letter to address his readers is "teknia". The word can lead one to think of their relationship to him; John regarded himself as their spiritual father. But the word for "children" in verse 14 is "paedia", also a diminutive, which can refer to children under tuition, instruction and discipline.

Another peculiar aspect of the above passage is the difference in the tenses used in verses 12 -14. In the Greek the verb "write" in verses 12 and 13 is in the present tense whereas in verse 14 the so-called aorist tense is used. Some Bible translators have translated verse 14 in past tense.

The two traits required of Christ followers, namely to keep his commands and to love one's neighbour can cause one to exclaim: "Who can do that?" (Romans 7:24). It helps us to be reminded of our new identity in Christ. We have received forgiveness of sins in the name of Jesus and have come to know the Father (John 14:9; 16:27). As we get to know him him better we come to realise Jesus is the one who "is and was and is to come" (Revelation 1:8). Furthermore, the Word of God enables us to be strong like young men, victorious over the evil one.

Three "age groups" seem to be addressed but another interpretation is possible: All followers of Jesus can be viewed as

> • "children" born again by believing in the name of Jesus through the preaching of the gospel,
> • "fathers" who have reached others by sharing their testimony,
> • "children" who are being brought up in the ways of their Creator,
> • "young men" who have overcome the evil one by the word of God which they have internalised.

# 8. Don't love this world (2:15-17)

15 Do not love the world or anything in the world. If anyone loves the world, love for the Father[d] is not in them. 16 For everything in the world—the lust of the flesh, the lust of the eyes, and the pride of life—comes not from the Father but from the world. 17 The world and its desires pass away, but whoever does the will of God lives forever.

{[d] or the Father's love}

Loving this world and its attractions is a threat to our friendship with God (James 4:4). The most loving human being who ever lived, innocent of doing anything wrong, was condemned to death by the Jewish Sanhedrin as well as a Roman court. Those were the most respected religious and legal institutions of the day. Is it any wonder that Paul said "the god of this world" was the devil (2 Corinthians 4:4)?

The way the world attracts us is through
1. what we feel and experience,
2. what we see and perceive and
3. what we think of ourselves.

The snake used this reality to tempt Eve. It worked and he got her to sin. He softened her up by sowing doubt about what exactly God had said about the tree – "did God say?" After he had got her engaged in conversation, he made God out to be a liar – "you will not surely die." In the end Eve gave in to the temptation (Genesis 3:1-6).

He used the same tactic to tempt Jesus when he fasted in the wilderness. Forty days after the voice from heaven had said "you are my beloved Son", satan tried to sow doubt in

Jesus' mind saying "If you are the Son of God ...". When that did not work he blatantly suggested that Jesus should intentionally ignore the first commandment and worship him. (Matthew 4:1-11.)

Like Eve, Jesus was tempted to satisfy the hunger of his body in a way God had not intended – "make bread out of these stones". But Jesus resisted with a quotation from the Law of Moses. The fruit from the tree of the knowledge of good and evil appealed to Eve's sense of pride – "desirable for gaining wisdom". Jesus, on the other hand, did not fall for the suggestion to show off by jumping from the roof of the temple.

The evil one was suggesting to Eve that the Lord was withholding something good from them. In the same way he promised Jesus authority over the kingdoms of the world. But Jesus knew that God had given the earth to man (Genesis 1:28). It was only by manipulating humans that satan got power over the kingdoms. Jesus' mission was to change the hearts of the people of these kingdoms by dying for them. In the end they will all surrender to him (Philippians 2:9-11).

The lure of the world has not changed since those days. Men still get distracted by "the girls, the gold and the glory". Buddhists realise this and strive to rid themselves of the desire for pleasure, possessions and power. If we want to live forever Jesus requires us to do the will of his Father (Matthew 7:21). This is not possible without his help (John 15:5).

# 9. Antichrists (2:18-20)

18 Dear children, this is the last hour; and as you have heard that the antichrist is coming, even now many antichrists have come. This is how we know it is the last hour. 19 They went out from us, but they did not really belong to us. For if they had belonged to us, they would have remained with us; but their going showed that none of them belonged to us. 20 But you have an anointing from the Holy One, and all of you know the truth.[e] {[e] or all things}

The term "antichrist" was used by John for the person Jesus called "the abomination of desolation spoken of by the prophet Daniel" (Matthew 24:15). When he stands in the holy place, Jesus said, those in Judea must flee to the mountains. Paul wrote about "the man of lawlessness, the son of perdition" who would be revealed. He would sit in the temple of God, displaying himself as a god before the "day of the Lord" would arrive (2 Thessalonians 2:3-4).

Throughout the ages Christians have longed for the return of the Lord. But first must come the defection or falling away (apostasia in Greek). So when "antichrists" were leaving the church John could have reckoned it was the "last hour".

Over the last century the world has drastically changed from "Christian" to secular. This is true for Europe and America as well as Russia. The Roman Catholic Church and the official state churches in the West as well as the orthodox churches in the East are far from perfect. Nevertheless, because of their influence, lawmakers have taken notice of the ethics, morals and values found in the Bible.

For centuries the vast majority of philosophers, scientists and authors held to the Judeo-Christian world view. But since the so-called age of enlightenment various factors brought about a transformation. The church of Rome was challenged by reformers at the same time that Copernicus (1473–1543) formulated the model of a heliocentric solar system. Galileo (1564–1642) was sentenced to indefinite imprisonment by the Roman Catholic Inquisition. That was because he supported the belief that the sun was the centre of our solar system, not the earth as taught by the Roman Church.

All these obvious flaws of Christendom may have given Descartes the courage to formulate his theories without reference to God. Scientists could not, and still cannot say with certainty how the world began. However, they could formulate and test theories without the mention of God. Napoleon was curious that Laplace (1749–1827) had not mentioned the Author of the universe in the book he had entitled: <u>Celestial Mechanics</u>. Laplace answered: "Sire, I had no need of that hypothesis". Napoleon told another scientist, Lagrange, who was a regular church attender. Lagrange remarked: "Ah, but that is a fine hypothesis. It explains so many things."

Jesus said false christs and false prophets will perform great signs and wonders to deceive, if possible, even the elect (Matthew 24:24). But every born-again believer has an anointing (chrisma in Greek) which helps him/her to differentiate between truth and falsehood.

# 10 Truth and lies (2:21-22)

21 I do not write to you because you do not know the truth, but because you do know it and because no lie comes from the truth. 22 Who is the liar? It is whoever denies that Jesus is the Christ. Such a person is the antichrist—denying the Father and the Son.

Ring of Truth is the name JB Phillips gave to his 1967 translation of the New Testament. He had begun translating while in a bomb shelter during Word War II. His aim was to produce a translation in modern English because the young people in his church did not understand the Authorised Version of the Bible.

In his memoir Ring of Truth: A Translator's Testimony Phillips said about the books of Matthew, Mark, Luke and John: "I have read, in Greek and Latin, scores of myths but I did not find the slightest flavour of myth here." He also said: "No man could ever have invented such a character as Jesus."

The religious leaders charged Jesus with blasphemy since he claimed to be the Anointed (Christ in Greek, Messiah in Hebrew). They handed him over to the Roman rulers by to be crucified. From their actions we can see why John called them antichrists.

However, the Jewish leaders were not the only ones who denied that Jesus was the Son of God. The first century world was dominated by Greek culture. Several Greek philosophers regarded matter as evil. In their thinking it was impossible that God would, or even could become a man. New converts of Greek background needed to turn their backs on their previous world view if they were to be true disciples of Jesus.

But some who had entered the church, among others a certain Cerinthus, came up with fanciful theology. They kept to the belief that matter was evil by making a difference between "the man Jesus" and the "Christ spirit" who supposedly entered Jesus at baptism and left him again before the crucifixion. Some of these people left the church because they did not belong there in the first place. John may have had Cerinthus in mind when he wrote about the liar and the antichrist.

The question of how the Creator could enter his creation dominated the thinking of church fathers during the early Christian era. In Genesis 3:16 God told the snake that the offspring of the woman would crush his head. The man is not mentioned in that context because the Saviour would be born without the participation of a man. The early church did not want to give false teachers a gap to deny Jesus' divinity. They went so far as to declare Mary the Theotokos which means "God-bearer". The term "Mother of God" is used in English. In 1854 the Roman Church announced the doctrine of the immaculate conception. This dogma declared that Mary was conceived and born without "original sin". Their reasoning was that the womb of the "Mother of God" had to be flawless and pure.

The Jehovah's Witnesses deny that Jesus is divine. John states that whoever denies the Son his rightful place is also insulting the Father. The early church formulated the so-called Nicean creed which declares that the Son is of the same substance as the Father. That means he is God.

# 11. Stay true (2:23-25)

23 No one who denies the Son has the Father; whoever acknowledges the Son has the Father also. 24 As for you, see that what you have heard from the beginning remains in you. If it does, you also will remain in the Son and in the Father. 25 And this is what he promised us—eternal life.

It is impossible to "have" the Father and at the same time claim that Jesus is a prophet or great teacher but not God. CS Lewis put forward a so-called trilemma, which can be summarised as follows:

"A man who was merely a man and said the sort of things Jesus said would not be a great moral teacher. He would either be a lunatic — on the level with a man who says he is a poached egg — or else he would be the Devil of Hell. Either this man was, and is, the Son of God: or else a madman or something worse. But let us not come with any patronising nonsense about His being a great human teacher. He has not left that open to us. He did not intend to." (Excerpt from Mere Christianity)

The early church relied heavily on the tradition handed to them by the apostles. They had the Old Testament scriptures and the word of mouth account about Jesus. It came from one of the twelve or Paul or someone properly instructed by them. Books were handwritten and therefore expensive. Church members had to memorise much of what was taught. Hence John's emphasis on "what you have heard from the beginning."

Throughout the ages God has made contact with man through progressive revelation. From the five books of

Moses one can trace the dealings of God with man over many centuries. The books of Moses are often quoted in the historic books (Joshua, Judges, Samuel, Kings …). None of the prophets of Israel disagreed with the books of Moses. They rather clarified and expanded topics of the Law, the name they gave to Moses' books. Jesus often quoted from the Law and the Prophets, never giving an indication that he doubted their truth. So did the authors of the New Testament.

After Jesus many have come with "new revelations" which disagree with the Bible. In the early church there were Cerinthus, Arius, Sabellius, Mani and more. Later came Mohammed and over the last two centuries Edward Irving (New Apostles) Ellen White (Seventh Day Adventists), Mary Baker Eddy (Christian Science), Joseph Smith (Mormons), Charles Russel (Jehovah's Witnesses) and many others.

The First Council of Nicaea was convened by the Roman emperor Constantine in 325. It produced the Nicaean Creed which is the first such document to be accepted by the vast majority of the congregations. More creeds were formulated in the centuries thereafter to make sure Christians kept to the correct interpretation of the apostles' teaching.

What we heard in the beginning when we dedicated our lives to following Jesus is what keeps us close to him. He promised us eternal life. No new "knowledge" can replace that.

# 12. Deceivers (2:26-29)

26 I am writing these things to you about those who are trying to lead you astray. 27 As for you, the anointing you received from him remains in you, and you do not need anyone to teach you. But as his anointing teaches you about all things and as that anointing is real, not counterfeit—just as it has taught you, remain in him. 28 And now, dear children, continue in him, so that when he appears we may be confident and unashamed before him at his coming. 29 If you know that he is righteous, you know that everyone who does what is right has been born of him.

Paul was concerened that certain "super apostles" were preaching a different Christ to the church in Corinth. He maintained that these preachers were charming them like the snake enticed Eve (2 Corinthians 11:3-5). He also warned the Ephesian elders that wolves would come from among themselves (Acts 20:29-30).

John was confident that the "anointing" his readers had received was the "real deal" and would help them decide whom to give their ears to. The word "anointing" is used a few times in 1 John. What exactly is meant by the word is not spelled out in the letter. What commentators agree on is that the anointing is what made a difference between those who "remain in him" and those who "went out from us". In the Greek the word is chrisma. It is formed from the root word chrio which means to anoint. Aso derived from chrio are Christos (Christ), christianos (Christian) and antichristos.

John was writing to assure true believers that their confidence in Jesus was well placed. He was also helping them to identify those who were preaching "another gospel". One of the ways in which false teachers distort the gospel is by claiming that the way to God is through the right knowledge. Usually their "knowledge" is obtained through so-called initiation. Sects of this kind can be classified as gnostic (knowledge is gnosis in Greek). The New Age movement is a modern day version of Gnosticism. Paul charged Timothy to guard what was entrusted to him and to turn away from contradictions, falsely called knowledge. (1 Timothy 6:20-21). Our faith is based on knowledge of the truth. Jesus said false prophets would rise up to lead astray even the chosen ones, if that were possible (Mark 13:22).

Christians are initiated into the body of Christ when we ask him to be the Lord of our lives. Whatever John meant by chrisma, Paul wrote that one could only belong to Christ if one had the Spirit of Christ (Romans 8:9). God's children have the ability to detect false promises because we are taught by his anointing (Romans 8:16). The believer's responsibility is to be faithful to Jesus so that we will not be caught off guard by his coming. He will come at a time when it is not expected (Matthew 24:42-51).

It would seem as if John did not want his readers to go on a witch hunt looking for false teachers. Famous people are often confronted by journalists to either be for or against someone. Jesus is the only human being who is worthy to confront us with that binary option. We are not called to have an opinion on the character of every church member. A transformed life which produces fruit of the Holy Spirit is proof of new birth (Galatians 5:22-23).

# 13. Children of God (3:1-3)

**3** See what great love the Father has lavished on us, that we should be called children of God! And that is what we are! The reason the world does not know us is that it did not know him. 2 Dear friends, now we are children of God, and what we will be has not yet been made known. But we know that when Christ appears,[a] we shall be like him, for we shall see him as he is. 3 All who have this hope in him purify themselves, just as he is pure. {[a] or when it is made known}

Some religions, and even some Christians, teach that all human beings are children of God. Paul quoted a Greek poet who said all humans were God's offspring. He did not oppose this belief because there is some truth in it. We have all been made in God's image. But Paul declared in the same breath that God commanded all to repent (Acts 17:28-30).

John was clearly thrilled by the idea that we could be called children of God. That happened when we received Jesus (John 1:12). The strange thing about Jesus' coming was that most of his own people rejected him. The leaders of the Jews were "of the world" and hated him because they did not know God. It has been a reality throughout the ages that most of the rulers of this world hate real Christians. This is true not only of political leaders but also of many religious leaders.

Outwardly we did not change when we were born from above. However, we know that Jesus followers also have the promise of an outward transformation. Paul called it our adoption or redemption of our bodies (Romans 8:23). Jesus was the son of David by birth (Matthew 1:1). He had always been the Son of God and the world was created by him (John 1:1; Hebrews 1:2). But he was declared the Son of God when he was raised from the dead (Romans 1:4). In this way he became the first-born among many brothers (and sisters) because he was the first human to have his body transformed, thereby becoming the first "heavenly man" (1 Corinthians 15:45-49). What awaits us is beyond our wildest dreams (1 Corinthians 2:9).

The Greek word for redemption can be interpreted the "deliverance obtained by a payment of ransom". Our ransom was paid on the cross. We were given the Spirit as down payment (Ephesians 1:13-14) but we will be freed of our old bodies when we see him. We already have new hearts spiritually but presently we are still "flesh and blood" which, according to Paul, cannot inherit the Kingdom of God (1 Corinthians 15:50). However, our new bodies will be immortal "flesh and bones" (Luke 24:39).

John uses the above facts to show the difference between God's children and those of the world. A child of God will make an effort to get rid of bad habits. Although salvation is free, those who put their hope in Jesus for the next life want to become more like him while in this mortal body. This they do because they appreciate the purity of Jesus who set himself apart (dedicated/consecrated/sanctified himself) so that he could be the perfect Lamb of God who takes away the sin of the world (John 17:19). When we get invited to a select event we dress for the occasion. How much more should we prepare for heaven!

# 14 Lawlessness (3:4)

4 Everyone who sins breaks the law; in fact, sin is lawlessness.

Law in the Bible usually means the books of Moses (Torah in Hebrew, Pentateuch in Greek). Jesus summed up the commands in these books with "love God and love your neighbour". The Jewish teachers of the law have found 613 commandments in the Torah. The Ten Commandments (Exodus 20: 3-17) form the basis for them all. Anyone who obeyed them completely would be a perfect human being. Another way to look at them is to say they describe the character of Jesus.

No society can function orderly without law. Even households must have rules so that the inhabitants have an idea of what to expect from one another. People who disregard physical laws must pay a price; think of gravity!

Countries have laws. Pascal made the observation that what's legally right or wrong can depend on which side of a river (boundary between countries) you find yourself. Nevertheless, for centuries the laws of Europe and its colonies were largely informed by the Bible. The erosion of the Judeo-Christian consensus started in Europe during the Enlightenment (approximately 1650 – 1850). The British commonwealth and America soon followed suit.

As the influence of the official European churches declined more and more thinkers came up with philosophies which did not mention God. Highly successful scientific theories gave rise to great technological advances. Intellectuals in the social sciences were hoping to copy the success of the physical sciences. However, when God is excluded from the discussion the concept of sin makes little or no sense. Most psychologists contradict sound Christian doctrine. They deny that every human being has tendency towards evil.

The revolution in philosophy reached a highpoint in the writings of Nietzsche (1844–1900). He used the phrase: "God is dead" and developed the philosophy of existential nihilism, according to which human life has no meaning, no purpose outside itself, or value in itself. But our human nature protests against meaninglessness as Victor Frankl discovered in a Nazi concentration camp. Some existentialists claim meaning can be found by making "a leap in the dark", a phrase coined by Kierkegaard (1813-1855).

People who said "No" to God, but wanted meaningful lives, have started some of the most depressing and destructive movements in politics (Marx), philosophy (Sartre), art (Picasso), film making (Woody Allen) and even theology (Feuerbach). It was prophesied by Jesus that society would be lawless in the last days due to a lack of love (Matthew 24:12).

Kenneth Latourette wrote in his book <u>Christianity through the ages</u> that secularism was a bigger threat to religion than communism. According to the journalist Malcolm Muggeridge "We have educated ourselves into imbecility". Francis Schaeffer was of the opinion that the two main values held by most 20th century people were "personal peace and affluence".

# 15. The Lost (3:5-6)

5 But you know that he appeared so that he might take away our sins. And in him is no sin. 6 No one who lives in him keeps on sinning. No one who continues to sin has either seen him or known him.

O f all the many works Jesus did, one act was foremost. He came to die for the sins of the world. Those who are saved by embracing this truth also believe that he was the only person who never sinned.

Jesus' enemies tried their utmost to pin some transgression of the law onto him but were not able. In the end they condemned him to death on the charge of blasphemy: he had dared to say he was the Son of God (Mark 14:61-64).

We who put our faith in the Lamb of God accept that only a person free of sin could pay for our sin. Our hearts belong to the One who saved us from destroying ourselves. Without him I would live with a guilty conscience or just ignore my conscience and get used to a sinful lifestyle. The next step would be to justify my life's choices. Many who do so then also want the whole world to tolerate and even commend their godless way of life.

Everyone who comes to faith in Christ receives a "new heart". The person's attitude to God is radically changed to a mindset of wanting to please his/her Saviour. Jesus said that remaining in him is the key to bearing fruit.

A person who lacks the desire to change his/her behaviour has never had a meaningful encounter with Jesus. This statement can give rise to speculations about election and predestination. The questions which arise are: "What about those who once professed to be saved but later took on a sinful lifestyle? Were such people never saved? Or did they lose their salvation?"

John did not theorise about the false teachers' claims of eternal security. He rather wanted to help believers to identify the deceivers. There are sects who teach that sinning in the body is quite acceptable for believers as long they we don't "sin in the spirit". In John's day there were those who believed their bodies were unimportant. They fell into two categories, typified by the Epicureans and the Spartans respectively. Since they attached little value to their bodies, Spartans treated their bodies with severity to make them fit for war. Epicureans, the opposite extreme, indulged their appetites to get maximum pleasure from their senses, like in the slogan: "Obey your thirst".

When one studies the Old Testament it becomes clear that God placed value on our bodies. Not only did he create us in his image, but he gave very specific instructions about food, hygiene and sexual relations. Jesus referred to his own body as a temple which was about to be torn down and rebuilt (John 2: 19, 21). Paul taught that a believer's body was a temple of the Holy Spirit (1 Corinthians 6:19). Jesus respected people's bodies by healing those who were diseased. If my body is the place where God lives with me, I should treat it with respect and care.

# 16. Jesus the conqueror (3:7-8)

7 Dear children, do not let anyone lead you astray. The one who does what is right is righteous, just as he is righteous. 8 The one who does what is sinful is of the devil, because the devil has been sinning from the beginning. The reason the Son of God appeared was to destroy the devil's work.

Bible verses are often quoted out of context and/or one-sided. One such passage is Jesus' advice about judging others. He did say "do not judge". However, in the same breath he added "do not give what is holy to dogs" (Matthew 7:1-6). He did not mean four-footed animals. In other words, we are allowed to make judgements about people who do good as well as those who lead lives which are blatantly sinful.

Just as in John's day there are people today who have been led astray to believe that their lifestyle has nothing to do with their faith. Paul instructed followers of Jesus not to associate or even to eat with any person who wanted to be known as a believer but who was leading a blatantly sinful life (1 Corinthians 5:9-11). Peter wrote in a letter to the churches that false teachers would be present among them (2 Peter 2:1). Jude warned that people who perverted grace into a licence for immorality had secretly slipped into the church (Jude 4).

God told Adam that he would die on the day that he sinned. It was the devil who tempted man to disobey. Now he accuses us before God (Revelation 12:10). In this way he has been sinning "from the beginning". In Hebrew he is known as satan which means opponent. John uses the Greek word is diabolos, a slanderer.

Jesus taught that those who kept on sinning were slaves to sin. In today's language: sin is addictive. The devil traps people in sin. The agents of secret services know that they can exploit the weaknesses of their opponents. They will tempt a government official to commit some shameful or illegal act. Then they will blackmail the person to betray his/her country by passing on secret information. Satan is a master at manipulating humans and keeping people in bondage. The angel Gabriel told Mary that her son should be called Jesus (Saviour) because he would save his people from their sins (Matthew 1:21).

The devil became notorious as the one who has power over death. When he entices one person to murder another, he can defend his prodding by saying all humans deserve to die anyway. But he made a big mistake when he became responsible for the death of the first human being who was truly innocent (John 13:2, 27). That proved his guilt beyond any doubt and now he stands condemned (John 16:11).

God had given mankind dominion over the earth and therefore a man was needed to take back the earth from satan's control. The Lion of Judah who is also the Lamb of God was the only one found worthy to open the seals of the book in Revelation 5:1-10. Some commentators have called it the "title deeds to the earth". He became a man in order to take away the power of the evil one who had kept humans in slavery (Hebrews 10:14-15). Jesus now holds the keys of death and hell (Revelation 1:18).

# 17. Children of the devil (3:9-10)

9 No one who is born of God will continue to sin, because God's seed remains in them; they cannot go on sinning, because they have been born of God. 10 This is how we know who the children of God are and who the children of the devil are: Anyone who does not do what is right is not God's child, nor is anyone who does not love their brother and sister.

Verse 9 makes more sense in Greek because of the subtlety of Greek grammar. But we know John is not talking about sinless perfection, because that would be contradicting what he had said in 1:8. As an illustration of the meaning of verse 9 consider the difference in attitude between a pig and a sheep when they fall into mud. The pig will enjoy it but the sheep will want to get out.

It is important distinguish between mistakes and sins. One can imagine the baby Jesus making mistakes. Maybe he fell in his first attempt to walk. Jesus scolded his disciples because they worried about a mistake they may have made (Mark 8:14-18). Not all mistakes are sins. Furthermore, temptation is not sin. Jesus was not ashamed to tell his disciples he was tempted by the devil in the desert. He was tempted in every way, just as we are (Hebrews 4:15).

According to Jesus the word of God is like seed. The seed is planted into hearts. Peter wrote that our new nature was generated by the living word of God which is seed that cannot perish (1 Peter 1:23). A person who is born-again treasures this seed which lasts forever inside of him/her. Jesus explained in the parable of the sower how different people treat the word (Luke 8:11-15). The people who value the word grow and become fruitful.

The Pharisees and teachers of the Law regarded themselves favoured by God, owing to the fact that they were
descendants of Abraham. But Jesus accused them of being
children of the devil, not Abraham, and of wanting to kill
him (John 8:37, 44). Before his conversion the zealous
Pharisee, Saul of Tarsus, persecuted the disciples of Jesus.
Jesus said that the time would come when those who kill
his followers would think they are doing God a favour.
(John 16:2). All this happens because of satanic deception.

The people who will ultimately be acknowledged as the
descendants of Abraham are those who have the same
faith as Abraham (Galatians 3:29). This does not mean
God has abandoned his plan for the Jews (Romans 11).
However, people who are born again, clean up their act.
The new person, having a "new heart", will strive to
please his/her new master. They use their bodies as instru-
ments of righteousness which means sin is no longer their
master (Romans 6:13-14).

Many passages in the New Testament encourage us to act
in a way one would expect of Christians. We already have
eternal life (John 5:24; Romans 8:1). Now we must live
like the new people we have become (Romans 8:12-13).

So far John has labelled those with false doctrine, denying
the divinity of Jesus, as antichrists and those who keep on
sinning as children of the devil. Here he states the most
important characteristic of all who belong to God, their
love for fellow believers. If that love is missing, the person
is not a child of God.

# 18. Murderers (3:11-15)

11 For this is the message you heard from the beginning: We should love one another. 12 Do not be like Cain, who belonged to the evil one and murdered his brother. And why did he murder him? Because his own actions were evil and his brother's were righteous. 13 Do not be surprised, my brothers and sisters,[b] if the world hates you. 14 We know that we have passed from death to life, because we love each other. Anyone who does not love remains in death. 15 Anyone who hates a brother or sister is a murderer, and you know that no murderer has eternal life residing in him.
{[b] the Greek adelphoi refers to males and females}

Again John emphasised the importance of remembering what they heard "from the beginning". Paul also encouraged believers to "hold on to the traditions you were taught" (2 Thessalonians 2:15). Jude wrote about the "faith that was once for all entrusted to God's holy people" (Jude 3). The message of salvation was not thought up by clever people; we received it from those who had also received it from others (2 Timothy 2:2). The heart of the gospel has not changed over the past 2000 years. The good news is still what Paul declared to the church in his first letter to the Corinthians, verses 1-4. This passage can be regarded as the first creed known to the early church.

Something else which has not changed since the days of Cain and Abel is the hatred of evildoers toward those who do good. Even Pilate realised that it was out of envy the Jewish leaders wanted Jesus killed (Matthew 27:18). Peter wrote that Christians were slandered because they did not go along with the sinful lifestyles of the people who did not know God (1 Peter 4:4).

Paul wrote about people "captive by satan to do his desire" (2 Timothy 2:26). God had told Cain that he should rule over the sin that was tempting him (Genesis 4:7) but Cain gave vent to his anger. His emotion overcame him in a moment but his hatred had been smouldering for a long time. Joseph's brothers had also hated him for some time before they decided to do him harm (Genesis 37).

Born-again believers have God's law written on their hearts (Hebrews 8:10). Our love for one another is proof that our spirits have been renewed. A person who lacks love for Christians must not claim to be born from above. In John's words, if anyone hates a believer that person is a murderer.

Jesus warned against unbridled anger (Matthew 5:21-22). Here is my understanding of what Jesus meant: If I hate someone so much that I wish him/her dead, and would cause the person's death if only I would not suffer any negative consequences (shame, prison, death sentence), then I am a murderer. In other words, if fear of retribution is the only thing keeping me from murder, I have already murdered in my heart. I do not yet sin if I have murderous thoughts toward someone. But if I don't get rid of those thoughts immediately, there is the possibility that in an unguarded moment I would commit a serious sin or even crime, just like Cain.

We can be sure that those of this world who hate us do not have eternal life. They are still "in death". This is another test believers can apply to discern if someone is from God.

# 19. Practical love(3:16-19)

16 This is how we know what love is: Jesus Christ laid down his life for us. And we ought to lay down our lives for our brothers and sisters. 17 If anyone has material possessions and sees a brother or sister in need but has no pity on them, how can the love of God be in that person? 18 Dear children, let us not love with words or speech but with actions and in truth. 19 This is how we know that we belong to the truth and how we set our hearts at rest in his presence:

When confronted with the challenge to love as Jesus loved it is normal to feel completely overwhelmed. Especially if one considers how Jesus loved as depicted in Philippians 2:5-8 and 1 Corinthians 13. But John quickly qualifies this statement by relating it to something with which anyone can identify. Even children understand the meaning of sharing although they are not always keen to do so.

There is more than one kind of love. When Paul wrote about the fruit of the Spirit, the first attribute he mentioned was love (Galatians 5:22-23). The kind of love John wrote about is not natural but something which grows in believers like fruit grows on trees. It is inspired by the Holy Spirit.

Jesus set the example of helping people in need and being compassionate to the marginalised. Peter commanded the cripple at the Gate Beautiful to get up and walk. He said that he gave the man that which he had, since he didn't have silver or gold. What Peter had was faith in Jesus. He believed God would do what he and John trusted him to do. He risked his reputation. We cannot command God to do our bidding. If the healing didn't take place Peter could be badmouthed and Jesus' reputation would suffer.

But how should we react if we don't have Peter and John's faith but we do have silver and gold? Should we still ask for miracles if we encounter needs which can be met by spending our money?

Jesus said in the Sermon on the Mount that we should give to the one who asks (Matthew 5:42). Although this should be our default attitude I don't think he meant it as a hard and fast rule. He did not allow himself to be co-opted into the agenda of those who followed him for material gain (John 6:26).

James singled out widows and orphans as worthy recipients of benevolence. The law of Moses commanded the people of Israel, no-one excluded, to care for the poor, the widows, the orphans and the strangers (immigrants) (Deuteronomy 15:7; Exodus 22:21-22). Paul encouraged Christians to do good to all, especially to those "of the household of faith" (Galatians 6:10). A believer who has no compassion for those who are suffering needs to question his/her commitment to Jesus.

Over the centuries Christians have cared for the sick and wounded, educated the poor, strived for the freeing of slaves, ended child labour and much more. When we help others practically our faith is strengthened and our hearts encouraged. Good deeds remind us whose children we are. We feel at ease in his presence when we do his will.

# 20. Sins of omission (3:20-24)

20 If our hearts condemn us, we know that God is greater than our hearts, and he knows everything. 21 Dear friends, if our hearts do not condemn us, we have confidence before God 22 and receive from him anything we ask, because we keep his commands and do what pleases him. 23 And this is his command: to believe in the name of his Son, Jesus Christ, and to love one another as he commanded us. 24 The one who keeps God's commands lives in him, and he in them. And this is how we know that he lives in us: We know it by the Spirit he gave us.

Most followers of Jesus often fail to obey him fully, especially his command to love our neighbours as ourselves. This can result in feelings or self-condemnation and unworthiness.

It is important for a believer to have a proper reaction to feelings of guilt. On the one hand we need to realise that self-condemnation is the enemy's way to rob us of our freedom in Christ (Romans 8:1). It is not Jesus' will that our good deeds are motivated by feelings of guilt.

On the other hand, our natural tendency is to find excuses for not caring for the less fortunate. We tend to blame our lack of love on circumstances, an organisation or a person. In this way we can deflect the uncomfortable feeling for a while but John recommends that we simply remind ourselves of the fact that God is "greater than our hearts".

Our confidence in God is restored by doing what pleases him. When the crowd who followed Jesus asked him how they should be serving God, he directed them to himself by saying "Believe in him whom he sent"(John 6:28-29). If we approach our Father like an innocent child we can expect to receive what we ask for.

If we believe in Jesus we will make it our business to study the things he commanded. He wanted Christians to be known by the love we have for one another (John 13:35). John did not tire of reminding his readers of this characteristic by which Jesus followers should be recognised. If Christians don't display love toward one another the world has a right to ask if Christianity "works".

Jesus said that he only spoke as the Father directed him (John 14:10). In the same way Jesus encouraged the apostles to remain in him and let his words remain in them (John 15:7). If we are continually conscious of the words of Jesus we are less likely to be self-centred. His words can also inspire us to motivate one another to acts of love and good works (Hebrews 10:24). That is one of the ways in which we "practice the presence of God", in the words of the Carmelite monk known as Brother Lawrence.

If anyone keeps God's commandments namely trusting in Jesus' name and loving fellow believers, that person will experience the presence of his Spirit. Before his departure Jesus said to his apostles: "I will ask the Father, and he will give you another advocate ... will not leave you as orphans" (John 14:16-18). He was referring to the Holy Spirit whom they would later receive. John wrote here that a believer would know the Spirit of God.

# 21. Test the spirits (4:1-3)

**4** Dear friends, do not believe every spirit, but test the spirits to see whether they are from God, because many false prophets have gone out into the world. 2 This is how you can recognise the Spirit of God: Every spirit that acknowledges that Jesus Christ has come in the flesh is from God, 3 but every spirit that does not acknowledge Jesus is not from God. This is the spirit of the antichrist, which you have heard is coming and even now is already in the world.

Beware of do-gooders who have no time for Jesus. The Israelites were warned not to be deceived into following other gods. Even a prophet or "dreamer of dreams" who correctly predicted events should not be listened to if that prophet had another agenda, namely to serve other gods (Deuteronomy 11:16; 13:1-3). Centuries later John warned against the many false prophets that were making their appearance in his day.

Paul warned the Christians not to lend their ears to those who were preaching what he called "another gospel". He meant a gospel different from the one they believed when they got saved. He even went so far as to pronounce a curse on an angel if the angel should proclaim a different gospel (Galatians 1:8). Satan can disguise himself to look like an angel of light (2 Corinthians 11:13-15). That should make us very careful of the people whose messages we listen to, including those who claim to have seen angels (Colossians 2:17).

Antichrists can be recognised by what they believe about Jesus (1 Corinthians 12:3). There are theologians who regard Jesus as the model human being. They say his example should be followed but they refuse to worship him as the Son of God. They are out to deceive others because they themselves are deceived (2 Timothy 3:13).

Judaism is not a study of the Old Testament but a certain interpretation of it. If John's test is applied to Judaism it is found to be an antichristian religion. It denies the Son of God his rightful place. Judaism should not be confused with Zionism which is a political movement. Most Zionists are not religious. But many religious people, including Jews and Christians, subscribe to Zionism. Christians base their support on the belief that God is keeping his promise to Abraham, namely that the land of Canaan would be an "everlasting possession" for his descendants. He repeated this promise to Abraham's son Isaac and to his grandson Jacob (Genesis 17:8; 26:3; 35:12). Christian supporters of Zionism also believe that many Old Testament prophesies must still be fulfilled in modern day Israel.

Zeitgeist is a German word for the concept "spirit of the age". It can be described as a spirit that dominates the politics, culture and fashions of an era. Believers need to be careful not to be swept up by popular movements. Paul warned that there would be "terrible times in the last days. People will be lovers of themselves ... having a form of godliness but denying its power." His instruction was to "have nothing to do with such people" (2 Timothy 3:1-5).

Antichristian "communities" (which are not communities) seek to create the impression of being like lambs but they speak like a dragon (Revelation 13:11). Communist and Fascist dictators claim to represent "the people" but don't allow freedom of speech.

## 22. The spirits of truth and of error (4:4-6)

4 You, dear children, are from God and have overcome them, because the one who is in you is greater than the one who is in the world. 5 They are from the world and therefore speak from the viewpoint of the world, and the world listens to them. 6 We are from God, and whoever knows God listens to us; but whoever is not from God does not listen to us. This is how we recognize the Spirit[a] of truth and the spirit of falsehood. {[a] or spirit}

Jesus told his apostles that they would be better off after he had left because the Holy Spirit could not come until he had been glorified (John 7:39; 16:7; Acts 2:33). Here John reminded his "children" of the Spirit who was in them. Paul felt the need to write to Timothy about the same truth (2 Timothy 1:7).

The Holy Spirit is promised to everyone who believes and is baptised (Acts 2:38-39). Among the manifestations of the Spirit is a gift known as "the discernment of spirits". Every Christian must expect to exercise this gift at some time or another. Jesus said his sheep recognise his voice (John 10:27). Spirits can originate from three sources namely God, the devil or a human. In Israel there were prophets who prophesied out of their own deceived hearts (Jeremiah 23:16; Ezekiel 13:2). They were well-meaning people who did not want to spread a "negative" message. They were telling the Israelites that all was well at a time when God wanted to wake them up to the danger they were in (Ezekiel 13:16).

Believers who find themselves threatened often use the phrase "greater is he that is in me than he that is in the world". In English the "you" in verse 4 could be singular or plural but the Greek is unmistakeably plural. From the context "dear children" and what follows it is clear that the discerning is not meant to be consigned to one person. There is safety in numbers (Proverbs 11:14). Paul instructed the church to judge prophesies (1 Corinthians 14:29).

Jesus called his followers "salt of the earth". A little bit of salt makes the food tasty. In this world true believers are a minority in most of the work places we find ourselves. At times we may find it a challenge to disagree with the views of those around us. It becomes especially hard when I am the only person with a worldview which is different from the view held by all the people I work with. I would feel peer pressure to conform. During such times it helps to gather with fellow believers regularly (Hebrews 10:25). We strengthen one another by corporate worship and listening to the preaching of truth. That is how we overcome (Revelation 12:11).

Ravi Zacharias spent his life defending the Christian faith. He was "totally convinced the Christian faith is the most coherent worldview around." Francis Schaeffer maintained that "Christianity is the greatest intellectual system the mind of man has ever touched". To quote John Lennox, Professor of Mathematics (emeritus) at the University of Oxford: "Either human intelligence ultimately owes its origin to mindless matter; or there is a Creator". Those who refuse God's offer of salvation are deaf to the very essence of truth (John 8:47). Paul warned that people would "turn their ears away from the truth and turn aside to myths" (2 Timothy 4:4; 2 Thessalonians 2:9-12).

# 23. The power of love (4:7-9)

7 Dear friends, let us love one another, for love comes from God. Everyone who loves has been born of God and knows God. 8 Whoever does not love does not know God, because God is love. 9 This is how God showed his love among us: He sent his one and only Son into the world that we might live through him.

Previously John wrote about light and life as qualities of God. Now he goes further by stating that love is the very nature of God. One cannot know him without knowing love and one cannot know love without loving. After creating Adam God said: "It is not good for man to be alone". The image of God in humans was incomplete before the creation of Eve. Loving relationships are what God is about and they are part and parcel of the new birth.

Probably the first Bible portion religious Jews teach their children to memorise is the so-called Sh'ma. It starts with "Hear O Israel" and continues with "love the LORD your God" (Deuteronomy 6:4-5). It would be unreasonable to expect a nation to love a God they cannot see and who has no interaction with them. But the ten commandments start with the words: "I am the LORD your God, who brought you out of Egypt" (Exodus 20:2). The departure from Egypt is commemorated every year at Passover to this day, more than three thousand years later.

Our love is a response to God's love which he shows over and over to his creatures. Not only were the Israelites led out of Egypt but God gave them food and water in the desert. Examples of God delivering his people are found in the accounts of Noah, Lot, Joseph, Moses, Gideon, David, Elijah, Hezekiah, Daniel and many, many more. David's response to God's acts of mercy and kindness can be read in many of the psalms in which he declares his love and adoration for his Saviour. David would have burned incense to the Lord in the holy place but he was not allowed to (2 Chronicles 26:16-21). One of the ways we can express our love for God is by worshipping as sincerely and energetically as David did (2 Samuel 6:12-19).

One of the consequences of humans being created in the image of God is our ability to choose. Many philosophers, psychologists and sociologists deny that we have a free will. They teach that all our actions are caused by neurons firing in our brains, and maintain that we have no control over which neurons are active; it is all predetermined by our genes and upbringing – nature and nurture. It is true that our free will is limited because we have been "sold as slaves to sin" (Romans 7:14). However, the concept of love is meaningless for beings without a measure of free will.

We have much more of a reason to love God than those who were saved from slavery in Egypt. Jesus lived among humans to show that God desired to be with us. He did not need to receive a baptism of repentance; he was sinless. But when he did, a voice was heard from heaven approving his decision. By getting baptised together with people who came to confess their sins Jesus in effect identified with sinful humans and was willing to pay the price needed to ransom us. If I were to disregard this superb act of intense love I would be saying NO to my Creator and his heaven.

# 24. The nature of love (4:10-12)

10 This is love: not that we loved God, but that he loved us and sent his Son as an atoning sacrifice for our sins. 11 Dear friends, since God so loved us, we also ought to love one another. 12 No one has ever seen God; but if we love one another, God lives in us and his love is made complete in us.

Nowhere in the gospels are we told if John had a wife or if he was romantically involved with someone. Those of us who have been married for a long time know that love is more than infatuation. Some psychologists say that the "honeymoon phase" can last up to 18 months. But there will be a stage in their relationship when two people who intend staying together as husband and wife need to have "hard conversations". If not, they risk losing the close connection they had at the beginning.

In our day the high rate of divorce among Christians is a sad reflection of a lack of commitment to Jesus. Eros is the Greek word for what may be termed hormone-assisted love. It is God-given and helps a couple to bond. Similarly the love of a mother for her child is aided by hormones to help her create a bond between them. But the Greek word agape is what John is referring to here. This kind of love may involve thinking and feeling but mainly involves one's will. It can require choices which do not appear or feel like the love popularly portrayed in Hollywood.

God demonstrated his love for mankind by sending his Son. We celebrate Christmas because we appreciate the fact that he came to live among us. Jesus is the giver of life. Those who refuse his love remain spiritually dead. But more important than Christmas is Easter. That is when we remind ourselves of the act by which we were forgiven so that we could obtain eternal life. How painful must it be for the Father to forgive us for killing his only Son? To fully appreciate our salvation we must acknowledge that Jesus had to die for us to be saved.

Listed among the gifts of the Spirit (1 Corinthians 12:28) is helps. This gift is often not appreciated as it should be. When the disciples gathered for the Last Supper not one of them volunteered to wash feet. Jesus demonstrated the love he had for them by doing this chore. He did so in spite of their insensitivity to the distress he was in.

Washing the disciples' feet was forerunner to the task which awaited him, that for which he was born. A more disgusting, revolting and distasteful assignment cannot be imagined. After Jesus was betrayed, his closest friends deserted him and the religious court found him guilty of a crime that deserved death. The civil court sentenced him to death by one of the cruellest means ever devised. The executioners decided to amuse themselves by humiliating and abusing him. All this he endured to secure salvation for everyone who would make use of it. A criminal who was crucified with him grabbed hold of this offer. He was convinced that Jesus would be the king of the world he was entering into after death (Luke 23:39-43).

John used the example of Jesus' love for us to illustrate the kind of love he was urging his readers to have for each other. I don't think Jesus was recommending that we wash people's feet as a ritual. The whole idea behind it is to do a distasteful chore for a brother or sister.

# 25. The presence of love (4:13-15)

13 This is how we know that we live in him and he in us: He has given us of his Spirit. 14 And we have seen and testify that the Father has sent his Son to be the Saviour of the world.

We experience the presence of God by means of his Spirit whom he has given us. John and the other apostles witnessed Jesus' teaching and miracles and also his death and resurrection. Jesus had promised them that his bodily absence would not disadvantage them.

When Philip asked Jesus to show them the Father, Jesus answered that he and the Father were one. The disciples had become very used to the presence of the Kingdom of God. It must have given them tremendous confidence to know they were close to Jesus; nothing seemed impossible. One can imagine their discomfort when he said he was not going to be with them much longer. They could be feeling like orphans, children who had lost their father. Jesus promised not to leave them as orphans but to ask the Father to send the Holy Spirit (John 14:16-18).

Parents can get "into the world" of a child by spending time with the child and communicating on a level the child can understand. We find it hard to believe that God would do that for us as individuals. But Jesus said whoever loves him will keep his word and experience the presence of both him and his Father (John 14:23). He elaborated on the work of the Spirit by saying the Spirit would lead them into all truth, foretell the future and glorify not himself but the Son (John 16:13-15). This agrees with what an angel later told John: "the testimony of Jesus is the spirit of prophesy" (Revelation 19:10).

The Greek word for spirit is pneuma. It can also mean wind or breath. God breathed into Adam and he became a "living soul" (Genesis 2:7). The Holy Spirit is promised to everyone who repents and is baptised in the name of Jesus Christ (Acts 2:38-39). There is disagreement among Christians about exactly when a believer receives the Holy Spirit. After his resurrection Jesus blew on his disciples and said to them "receive the Holy Spirit" (John 20:22).

However, just before his ascension he also told them not to leave Jerusalem before being "clothed with power from on high" (Luke 24:49). According to Luke his last words to his disciples were: "You shall receive power when the Holy Spirit comes upon you and you shall be my witnesses..." (Acts 1:8). John was doing just that in this letter, witnessing about Jesus. He declared to those who confessed that Jesus was the Son of God that God was with them. If we ask our Father for the Holy Spirit, we can know for certain that no other spirit would enter us (Luke 11:13).

Paul appealed to believers to keep on being filled with the Spirit (Ephesians 5:18) and also to "walk in the Spirit" (Galatians 5:16). Then he listed the fruit of the Spirit (Galatians 5:22-23). The Spirit of God is a Spirit of love. While we are filled with the Spirit we will bear the fruit which can be expected from someone who "remains in the vine" which is Jesus (John 15:1-8).

# 26. Perfect love (4:16-19)

16 And so we know and rely on the love God has for us. God is love. Whoever lives in love lives in God, and God in them. 17 This is how love is made complete among us so that we will have confidence on the day of judgment: In this world we are like Jesus. 18 There is no fear in love. But perfect love drives out fear, because fear has to do with punishment. The one who fears is not made perfect in love. 19 We love because he first loved us.

Having been witnesses of Jesus' sacrificial death and resurrection must have overwhelmed the apostles. At first they must have been in severe shock. But later they were stirred with a sense of God's love. How could they forget the words: "This is my body" and "This is my blood" when they saw the reality of it the next day?

Love reaches perfection when I am so convinced of God's love that nothing can disturb my tranquillity. God did not give us a spirit of fear ... (1 Timothy 1:7); his peace passes all understanding (Philippians 4:7). Together with faith and hope love is everlasting (1 Corinthians 13:13). In the day of judgement we can be as sure of God's love as we ever were here on earth.

Those who reject such a display of love as was revealed by Jesus have reason to fear (Hebrews 2:3). Also, when we as believers on occasion act without love (and who doesn't), we may experience fear. Fearing God is appropriate when we disobey him; ideally every believer must continually "remain in him". Some of Bob Dylan's songs may very well have been inspired by the behaviour of immature Christians. He addressed them in song with the words:

"Do you ever wonder just what God requires? You think He's just an errand boy to satisfy your wandering desires." Solomon already noticed that unanswered prayer can lead to depression, a very common condition in the 21st century (Proverbs 13:12).

Just as there are people born with physical disabilities, some have a predisposition to depression and anxiety. There are also those who have been damaged by their up-bringing and become self-centred as a consequence. We live in the age of selfies. Paul wrote that in the last days people would be lovers of themselves (2 Timothy 3:2).

Nowhere did Jesus encourage us to love ourselves. Yet the media tell us we don't love ourselves enough! Self-harm is one of the "diseases" of the 21st century. An older man when questioned on why he cut himself said "it's because the pain you've got and it brings it out of you instead of holding it in" (EClinicalMedicine 12 (2019) 52). That is not an indication of self-hatred as some may assume.

John reminded his readers that their love resulted from their knowledge of God's love for them. My love is not perfect because my knowledge of his love for me is not complete. Jesus is with us here and he will also be with us when we die (2 Corinthians 5:8). We may experience the discipline of the Lord, in fact, we will (Hebrews 12:7-8). But we must not fear that he is punishing or condemning us (John 5:24; Romans 8:1).

# 27. Real and fake love (4:20-5:1)

20 Whoever claims to love God yet hates a brother or sister is a liar. For whoever does not love their brother and sister, whom they have seen, cannot love God, whom they have not seen. 21 And he has given us this command: Anyone who loves God must also love their brother and sister.

5 Everyone who believes that Jesus is the Christ is born of God, and everyone who loves the father loves his child as well.

Some very religious people are filled with hatred. There are those who have convinced themselves that their hatred is born out of a love for God. John calls them liars. There is a difference between someone who lies occasionally and someone who is a liar, just as having once stolen something does not make that person a thief.

John's logic can be understood by remembering how Jesus explained to Nicodemus that only born-again people were able to see the Kingdom of God. He made use of wind as an illustration of the Spirit. One cannot see the wind, only its effect. In the same way one cannot judge someone else's love for God other that by seeing it displayed in his/her love for fellow believers.

Many influential leaders, including Mahatma Gandhi, have said that they admire Jesus but not his church. Through the ages atrocities have been committed in the name of Christianity. Thomas More, Lord Chancellor of England (a man for all seasons) became so obsessed by his conflict with William Tyndale (Bible translator) that he did not rest before he had him arrested and burnt at the stake. Thomas More in turn was executed by Henry VIII for refusing to acknowledge king Henry as head of the church. We have a right to question if people like Thomas More or Henry VIII were genuine believers.

The internet has become a free-for all medium which some Christians are using to malign other Christians who happen to have an interpretation of the Bible different from their own. Seekers, agnostics, atheists and those who are of a different religion are put off from Christianity by this lack of respect among those who profess Christ. The tragedy is that seekers could lose out on eternal life. By refusing to associate with people they regard as bigots and hypocrites, they never honestly investigate the claims of Christ.

James warned those who wanted to teach other Christians that they would be judged by a stricter standard than an "ordinary" believer (James 3:1-2). This is because what they teach can affect their hearers' eternal destiny. We all say things which would have been better unsaid. Everyone with influence must take extra care of what he/she says.

Absalom murdered his half-brother Amnon. Their father David had not acted against Amnon for raping his sister. Later Absolom's hatred for their father was revealed when he tried to grab hold of the kingdom through an armed uprising (2 Samuel 13:22-23, 28-29; 15:10-14). Similarly, someone who hates a child of God but claims to love God is a liar. Sometimes Christians encounter their greatest opposition from other Christians. They could be tempted to justify hatred toward their perceived enemy. John maintains that their so-called love for God is not genuine. Anyone who professes love for Jesus should love all the children of God.

# 28. The power of faith (5:2-4)

2 This is how we know that we love the children of God: by loving God and carrying out his commands. 3 In fact, this is love for God: to keep his commands. And his commands are not burdensome, 4 for everyone born of God overcomes the world. This is the victory that has overcome the world, even our faith.

When fellow believers act in an unloving manner we may not feel affectionate toward them. This could cause us to doubt if our love for them is authentic. Jesus told the apostles to forgive a brother or sister who sinned against them seven times in a day if they also apologised seven times. Their response was: 'Increase our faith!' (Luke 17:3-5). If we love God and keep his commands we can set our hearts at ease that our love is real.

The bulk of the teachings of Jesus can be found in the so-called Sermon on the Mount (Matthew 5-7). One could be forgiven for regarding his instructions as burdensome. For instance, to enter the Kingdom of Heaven, he said one needed to be more righteous than the teachers of the law (rabbis). Yet, he claimed that his yoke was easy and his burden light (Matthew 11:30). "Yoke" was a term in use by the teachers of the Bible (Old Testament) for what they regarded as God's requirements.

All religions besides Christianity require their adherents to earn the favour of God or their gods. Those who do the needed rituals are rewarded, whether in this life or in the afterlife. People under the yoke of such religions are full of superstitions, always afraid some misfortune will befall them. But Jesus came that we may have abundant life (John 10:10).

It is possible to be more righteous than the religious elite who claim to keep the 613 laws they found in the Bible. This is so because righteousness based on keeping God's commands cannot justify anyone before him. No-one other than Jesus has been able to keep his commands without committing a single sin. By believing in Jesus a person is born again (John 1:12-13). The only way to be declared "not guilty" by God and enter the Kingdom of Heaven is to trust in the sufficiency of Jesus' death and re- surrection (Romans 10: 13; 1 Corinthians 1:30).

The message of the Sermon on the Mount was summed up by Jesus in his version of the Golden Rule (Matthew 7:12). Many wise men have given their followers this rule but only Jesus gave it a pro-active formulation. Moreover, he gave his followers the Holy Spirit to assist us in keeping it. We need to always be alert not to fall back into trying to earn God's favour. Neither should we put burdens on the shoulders of other believers to keep all kinds of rules not found in the New Testament. Jesus berated the Phar- isees for this practice (Matthew 23:4).

The world of John was dominated by the mighty Roman Empire. He claimed that the faith of the believers had overcome the world. He may have had a prophetic inkling of the fact that Christianity would be declared the official religion of the Roman Empire in 380AD, less than 300 years later.

# 29. The three witnesses (5:5-8)

5 Who is it that overcomes the world? Only the one who believes that Jesus is the Son of God. 6 This is the one who came by water and blood—Jesus Christ. He did not come by water only, but by water and blood. And it is the Spirit who testifies, because the Spirit is the truth. 7 For there are three that testify: 8 the[a] Spirit, the water and the blood; and the three are in agreement.

{[a] in the Vulgate there is more to this verse}

Each of the letters to the seven churches in Revelation contain a promise to "the one who overcomes". Here the enemy who is conquered by believers is named. It is "the world". Jesus told his apostles that he had overcome the world (John 16:33). Earlier in this letter John told of the danger of loving the world. The ruler of this world will tempt us, threaten us and try to seduce us but we conquer by our faith in Jesus.

Some say they believe in Jesus, but do they believe he is the Son of God? On the one hand sonship means that he has the nature of God. The early church explained this fact in a creed saying he was "of the same substance as the Father". On the other hand he "came by the water and the blood".

Everyone familiar with Old Testament scripture knows the reason why Israelites were forbidden to eat blood, namely "the life is in the blood". The same ban applies to converts from non-Jewish nations (Acts 15:20, 29). Blood was not called "unclean" like pork or shellfish. Students of medicine know that every part of the body is nourished by blood. When Jesus shed his blood he gave the very essence of his life to anyone who would accept it. He taught the congregation in Capernaum they could only have eternal life if they ate his flesh and drank his blood. When they started grumbling he explained that he did not mean them to become cannibals (John 6:53-57, 63).

There were and still are those who refuse to believe that God would live among people on earth. Paul's letter to the Colossians was aimed at countering their influence. By saying that the Christ came only by water, the so-called Gnostics alleged that the "Christ spirit" descended on the man Jesus when he was baptised in water. Under this anointing (chrisma) he supposedly had the power to do miracles. But according to them the "Christ spirit" left the man Jesus before he was crucified. To the Gnostics it was inconceivable that humans could kill the Son of God.

On the day of Pentecost the Spirit came upon the believers who were expecting him. Peter preached a sermon under the anointing of the Spirit, testifying that God had made Jesus "Lord and Christ" (Acts 2:36). When Jesus referred to himself he often used the term Son of Man. In Paul's words he is the second man who is also the last Adam (1 Corinthians 15: 45-46). In him the fullness of the deity dwells bodily (to this day) (Colossians 2:9).

When believers get baptised we remember that he came by water. We celebrate holy communion to remember he also came by blood. When we receive the Holy Spirit we have power to be his witnesses. If Jesus' disciples and the early Christians received the Gift of the Holy Spirit after conversion, is it not reasonable for all believers today to expect the same Gift (Acts 8:14-17)?

# 30. The testimony of God (5:9)

9 We accept human testimony, but God's testimony is greater because it is the testimony of God, which he has given about his Son.

When Jesus was baptised a voice from heaven was heard testifying that he was the Son of God. The Holy Spirit descending on him in the form of a dove was also testimony of his divinity.

A voice spoke from heaven again just before Jesus said he would draw all people to himself through his death on a cross (John 12:27-32). During the last few months of his life on earth Jesus put a lot of effort into drawing attention to himself. He promised living water to those who dared to believe in him (John 7:37-38). He claimed to be the light of the world (John 8:12) and also to have been alive before Abraham (John 8:58).

When Moses asked God for his name the Lord answered "I AM" (Exodus 3:14). In Hebrew this is written YHWH, the so-called tetragrammaton. Religious Jews regard this word as too holy to pronounce. Where it occurs in the Bible they read "Adonai" or "Hashem". In most English Bibles the word is translated LORD – capital letters to distinguish it from other names used for God. On the occasion when Jesus used the words "Before Abraham was I am" the Jews picked up stones to kill him (John 8:58). This was because he applied the words "I am" to himself.

Jesus could hardly have used more outlandish language to claim that he was God than "I and the Father are one" (John 10:30). The Jewish council condemned him to death because of this claim (Luke 22:66-71). Anyone living in the first century could find ample witnesses who would affirm that Jesus regarded himself as the Son of God.

Most twenty-first century people have access to enough evidence that the first believers in Jesus formed a sizeable congregation in Jerusalem. It is also very well documented that members of the early church refused to call Caesar Lord because they claimed that Jesus was Lord. For this many paid with their lives. Several modern theologians who don't believe in the resurrection nevertheless agree that 1 Corinthians 15:3b-5 was a creed, an early Christian statement of faith.

People who believe the Bible is true are often made out to be stupid and ignorant. Most followers of Jesus were not persuaded to believe in him by studying the historical evidence of his resurrection. Rather, we were convicted of our sin and our need of a Saviour. This does not mean our decision was uninformed, or that we took a "leap in the dark". We responded to a prompt from the Holy Spirit. Some sceptics will brush it off as an emotional decision, "not based on reality".

But emotions are real. What is invisible is not necessarily unreal. Most people make many ordinary day decisions based on emotion. This fact is well documented in the book of Nobel laureate Daniel Kahneman: Thinking, Fast and Slow. Regarding the resurrection JB Phillips wrote: "As I pressed on with the task of translation I came to feel utterly convinced of the truth of the resurrection". Since we cannot interview eyewitnesses about the truth of the gospels we rely on human testimonies regarding them.

# 31. The truth about God (5:10)

10 Whoever believes in the Son of God accepts this testimony. Whoever does not believe God has made him out to be a liar, because they have not believed the testimony God has given about his Son.

One of the sayings of AW Tozer was: "What I believe about God is the most important thing about me".

There was a time when I was debating in my mind on whether I wanted to believe there was a God. I looked for reasons not to believe because I did not want to be held accountable for some of the things I had done. It is hard to be honest with yourself when you know honesty puts you in a bad light. I suppressed thinking about Jesus or God most of the time.

It is easy to find a reason not to believe in an almighty God who is also all loving. The argument is simple but philosophers have debated it for millennia. A theodicy is an attempt to justify the existence of evil, while an omni-benevolent God who is also omnipotent looks on. It is also known as Epicurus's trilemma. Plato wrote about this paradox as did Augustine and many before and after them.

Francis Schaeffer attributed to the French Philosopher Baudelaire the saying: "If there is a God, he is the devil". If Baudelaire really said that he must have given up on the idea of God being good. It is understandable that Jews find it hard to forgive God for allowing the Holocaust. There are those who say God is not almighty. They don't believe he is able to do away with evil. Greek philosophers connected evil to the material world. They avoided the idea of an omnipotent God by believing in many gods. Many religions make this assumption.

One of the bothersome questions I had while searching for meaning in my life was the one Judas Iscariot asks in the play Jesus Christ Superstar: "Jesus Christ Who are you? What have you sacrificed?" If I were to believe this person who radiated goodness was crucified simply because he was at the wrong place at the wrong time, could I then expect my life to have meaning? And I wanted my life to have meaning. That decision started me on a path to find the Truth. The only meaning I could logically ascribe to Jesus' death was that it was meant to draw my attention and that it was for my sin.

Many who call themselves atheists have set themselves up as judges of God. They decided that what is known of God is repugnant to them. The title of the posthumous book by CS Lewis, God in the Dock, says it all.

Atheist philosophers like Sartre end up at a place where they don't believe that our lives have meaning. That is why he could write: "Man is condemned to be free" which led him to say "Every man must invent his own path". John says these people are calling God a liar. According to them the Galilean Jesus didn't do enough to convince them of God's existence and benevolence!

An honest seeker could be surprised by the conclusion of someone like former atheist and investigative journalist Lee Strobel (https://leestrobel.com/). The evidence to prove that Jesus rose from the dead is better documented than the evidence needed to prove Julius Caesar existed.

# 32. Eternal life (5:11-12)

11 And this is the testimony: God has given us eternal life, and this life is in his Son. 12 Whoever has the Son has life; whoever does not have the Son of God does not have life.

According to John Wesley (1703-1791 the witness of the Spirit is "an inward impression on the soul, whereby the Spirit of God directly witnesses to my spirit, that I am a child of God; that Jesus Christ hath loved me, and given Himself for me; and that all my sins are blotted out, and I, even I, am reconciled to God".

I remember a colleague calling me a "time glutton". That was because I wanted a longer life than just what we were allotted on earth. A young man came to Jesus with the same desire (Mark 10:17-22). The man led an exemplary life in which he also seemed to be successful. But he was not sure about his eternal destiny. He desperately wanted to make sure he would be counted among the "righteous", those who would live forever.

Thousands, if not millions of people living today should similarly consider themselves rich, young and "ruling".

Jesus loved him and wanted the very best for him, but his criteria for discipleship were much stricter than the man had anticipated. Jesus is not happy to be an "add on" to our lives. From the very first words he spoke to the end of the conversation his intention was to get this fact across.

Firstly, Jesus was not opposed to the ruler calling him "good", as long as he was willing to acknowledge that the attribute "good" belongs exclusively to God. Then, as a

kind of teaser he referred the man to the upbringing he
must have had in a Jewish household. He must have learnt
"the Law". When asked "which commandments" Jesus
conspicuously omitted the "first table" commandments
which relate to God. He only quoted the commandments
which refer to our behaviour towards other humans. But
he also excluded the last command of the "second table":
"You shall not covet ...". Greed is a form of idolatry which
is harmful to our relationship with God (Ephesians 5:5).

Finally the young man was ready to receive the clincher:
"Give up your present life and follow me". If he could put
two and two together he would notice that Jesus implied
following him would be equivalent to complying with the
commandments relating to God. In other words, Jesus was
making a not too subtle claim of divinity.

The immediate benefit of following Jesus would be the
promise of an eternal "treasure in heaven". What a bar-
gain! The man went away sad but had much to meditate
on: Did he really prefer an eternal treasure to earthly
treasures? We do not know if he afterwards heard of Jesus'
death and alleged resurrection. Was he perhaps among
the three thousand who came to faith in Jesus on the day
of Pentecost?

No-one other than God is eternal. Eternal life consists in
knowing God (John 17:3). Christ gives eternal life as a
gift to those the Father gave to him (John 17:2). This
world is fleeting and we should set our hope fully on what
is to come (1 Peter 1:13). Nevertheless, every believer
must expect an abundant life here and now (John 10:10).

# 33. Assurance of salvation (5:13)

13 I write these things to you who believe in the name of the Son of God so that you may know that you have eternal life.

The motivation for writing the fourth gospel is stated in the second last chapter (John 20:31). John gave the same reason for writing his first pastoral letter. But here he adds the word "know". He asserted that I can know that I am a child of God and have eternal life.

Much controversy has surrounded this truth through the ages. For centuries the writings of Augustine (354-430) were held in such high esteem that his theology was widely accepted. His understanding of election and pre-destination formed a significant part of his famous book City of God. In there Augustine put forward his doctrine of "original sin".

It has been doctrine of the Roman as well as Protestant churches that we all inherit an "Adamic" nature which is prone to sin. Augustine's view was that this "original sin", with which all are born, deserved punishment. He formulated this doctrine to refute Pelagius (354-418) who taught that babies were born innocent. Pelagius said that man's free will enabled him to obey the commands of God, whereas Augustine insisted that this was impossible without God's enabling grace. Eventually Pelagius was condemned as a heretic by the Council of Ephesus in 431.

An important aspect of the Augustine – Pelagius polemic was the matter of baptism. Pelagius did not regard baptism in water as essential for salvation but Augustine did. Augustine held that "original sin" was taken away by the "sacrament" of baptism. But baptism would not guarantee salvation; only the elect would be given the ability to persevere to the end. In A Treatise on Rebuke and Grace he wrote "who...can presume... that he is in the number of the predestinated?" John Stott disagreed. Commenting on 1 John 5:13 he wrote "certainty and humility do not exclude one another" and furthermore "presumptuousness lies in doubting God's word".

Calvin regarded baptism as a sign of the covenant between God and his people, not an action which could wash away sin. The Reformed churches teach that circumcision, the sign of the Old Covenant, was replaced by baptism. That baptism in itself does not cleanse from sin is clearly correct (1 Peter 3:21). However, neither Jesus nor the apostles made any connection between baptism and the New Covenant. The ideal occasion for the apostles to have said baptism replaced circumcision, if they believed it did, would have been at the Jerusalem Council described in Acts 15. Holy Communion is associated with the New Covenant (Matthew 26:28; 1 Corinthians 11:25).

Luther's contribution to followers of Jesus can be summed up in his favourite verse "The just shall live by faith". This verse from Habakkuk 2:4 is quoted 3 times in the New Testament. He vehemently opposed the prevailing Roman Catholic doctrine according to which good works made a contribution to salvation. Luther obtained for himself the assurance that he was a child of God and wanted every believer to have that same assurance of sins forgiven, a clear conscience and peace with God. 1 John 5:13 is a verse that has greatly helped me in times of doubt.

# 34. Our confidence (5:14-15)

14 This is the confidence we have in approaching God: that if we ask anything according to his will, he hears us. 15 And if we know that he hears us—whatever we ask—we know that we have what we asked of him.

Christians often wonder why their prayers are not granted. If I pray "in Jesus' name", can I not expect an affirmative answer? But John makes it clear that the request has to be according to his will.

When we pray in Jesus' name we are asking his Father for that which Jesus gave us the authority to ask (John 15:16). Jesus can delegate authority since all authority was given to him before he ascended into heaven (Matthew 28:18).

Books have been written on why we don't always receive from God what we ask. We don't necessarily know if the answer is "yes", "no" or "later". If it is in God's will to grant our request we often have to exercise patience. Sometimes God wants us to persevere in prayer. Jesus taught this in the parable of the widow and the unjust judge (Luke 18:1-8) and modelled it in the case of the Canaanite woman (Matthew 15:21-28). He commended the woman for her great faith. Tenacity in prayer is a sign that the requester has faith.

Daniel prayed 21 days before he obtained a visit from heaven (Daniel 10:12-13). If I firmly believe my wish is in his will, and if it is an urgent matter, I will surely continue to pray till I get the answer. In his letters Paul encouraged his readers to be praying at all times (Romans 12:12; Ephesians 6:18; 1 Thessalonians 5:17).

Much has been speculated and written about God's will. Jesus asked his disciples to pray that our Father's will should be done (Matthew 6:18). That prayer would not have been necessary if his will was always done, as some people believe and teach. It is not God's will that anyone should perish (2 Peter 3:9) but we know some will go lost (John 17:12).

Our minds find it incomprehensible that Almighty God allows bad things to happen against his will. This paradox can to some extent be explained by accepting that every human being, made in the image of God, also has a will. When my will is in conflict with that of my Creator, he often lets me have my way. Hopefully I shall learn from my mistakes. But having "my way" will harm my relationship with God. It can also cause great pain to others as well as to myself.

Human parents may also let a child have its way, even against their will. But well informed parents know that it is not good to give in to a young child's every whim. In the same way, there is a danger that God's children can become ungrateful if he immediately complied with our every request (Romans 1:21)

It is instructive to read about Paul's determination to do God's will contrary to his friends' wishes (Acts 20:22-24; 21:4, 10-14). Jesus knew he would be crucified but did not flinch from going to Jerusalem. It would seem as if Jesus' will was not the same as that of his Father's when he prayed in the Garden of Gethsemane (Luke 22:42). We should be eternally thankful that he did his Father's will.

# 35. Peter and Judas (5:16-17)

16 If you see any brother or sister commit a sin that does not lead to death, you should pray and God will give them life. I refer to those whose sin does not lead to death. There is a sin that leads to death. I am not saying that you should pray about that. 17 All wrongdoing is sin, and there is sin that does not lead to death.

Jesus taught persistence in prayer in the Sermon on the Mount (Matthew 7:7-11). It was in the context of the wisdom needed to judge others. He encouraged generosity (verse 12) but not blind stupidity (verse 6). James wrote that God would give wisdom to those who ask in faith (James 1:5).

John was at the last supper where Jesus warned Peter that he would deny him. Satan had requested to sift the apostles like wheat (Luke 22:31). When wheat is sifted the chaff blows away; only what is useful remains. Judas was not going to remain and Peter would find out that his overconfidence was not enough to save him from acting cowardly.

Jesus was troubled in spirit that one of his apostles would betray him. It seems as if only that man and Jesus knew his identity. Judas had already agreed with the chief priests to betray him. While Jesus was eating his last meal with the twelve, satan entered Judas who then went out (John 13:27, 30).

It is comforting to know that Jesus told Peter he had prayed for him. If Peter had given up on believing in Jesus, would there be Christians today? But Jesus prayed that his faith would not fail so that he could afterwards encourage his brothers.

All the apostles echoed Peter's promise of loyalty. In the garden of Gethsemane Jesus warned them again that they should pray in order not to fall into temptation. They did not manage. They must have been emotionally drained.

When their test came all abandoned Jesus.

John could very well have reflected on these events when he wrote about a sin that does not lead to death and sin that leads to death. Would Peter have chosen life if Jesus had not prayed for him? He burst out crying when he heard the cock crow and realised he had failed. Judas chose physical death by his own hand. He had already committed a sin that led to spiritual death by preferring thirty pieces of silver over friendship with the Son of God.

"Follow your heart" is a common recommendation in 21st century Hollywood culture. But our hearts can deceive us (Jeremiah 17:9). Peter found out the hard way. The media and educational institutions propagate a plethora of lies, as prophesied by Paul (2 Thessalonians 2:11-12). Many don't know their right hand from their left (Jonah 4:11). The devil would destroy every Christian's faith if possible. But God puts us in communities where we can pray for our friends who fall into sin (James 5:19-20).

# 36 Sinners and saints (5:18-19)

18 We know that anyone born of God does not continue to sin; the One who was born of God keeps them safe, and the evil one cannot harm them. 19 We know that we are children of God, and that the whole world is under the control of the evil one.

Here John helps his readers to identify those among them who are not children of God. If a new convert remains in a sinful lifestyle we have the right to ask if a new birth did in fact occur. Some people take longer to part with their bad habits than others. Paul accused the Corinthians of lacking maturity and needing to be treated like babies. He nevertheless addressed them as brothers and sisters, children of God (1 Corinthians 3:1). However, Jesus warned against those who were leaders but did not clean up their act, calling them wolves in sheep's clothing (Matthew 7:15-16).

On their way to Gethsemane Jesus prayed for those the Father had given him, those who accepted his words and believed that the Father had sent him. He asked for their protection as well for ours, who believed in him through their message (John 17:2, 8, 15, 20). In this letter John asserts that the Son of God keeps us safe. If we remain in him, he is able to keep us (Jude 20-24).

All the children of God on earth can be considered as members of the same tribe. In his letters Paul addressed believers as saints (Romans 1:7, 1 Corinthians 1:2 etc). The most common attack of satan against us is to divide us. That gives him the opportunity to plant "secret agents" among us who "work for the other side". Jesus prayed for his followers to be united (John 17:20-21).

Unity is not the same as uniformity. If the twelve apostles were to engage in discussions on politics they would have been likely to have different persuasions. Imagine Simon the Zealot debating politics with Levi the tax collector!

Our struggle is not against other people but against evil cosmic powers (Ephesians 6:12). It is not popular in the 21st century to insist that "we know". In this so-called scientific age we are frowned upon for claiming to know any truth other than that which can be "scientifically proven". Most people who use such terminology have been brainwashed into believing everything communicated by popularisers of science such as Carl Sagan.

Many so-called experts preach the religion of Scientism which is not verifiable or falsifiable by repeatable experiments. The title of a book by author James M Rochford, Evidence Unseen: Exposing the Myth of Blind Faith, is an indication of the fact that our faith is not ""blind". Proof "beyond reasonable doubt" can be supplied to anyone who is open to investigate it.

The words "under the control" in verse 19 do not appear in the Greek, a fact which is supported by other English translations. The earth was not given to satan but to mankind (Genesis 1:28; Psalm 8:6; Hebrews 2:6). Humans, world leaders in particular, can be manipulated by the devil. That is how the whole world continues to "lie in the evil one". Eventually satan worship will be commonplace (Revelation 13:4).

# 37. Idols (5:20-21)

20 We know also that the Son of God has come and has given us understanding, so that we may know him who is true. And we are in him who is true by being in his Son Jesus Christ. He is the true God and eternal life. 21 Dear children, keep yourselves from idols.

Knowing a person involves much more than knowing a fact. Jesus claimed to be the truth, a statement which sounds bizarre in most ears. It must be understood in the light of two other claims, namely that he has life in himself and that he is the door to knowing our Creator (John 5:26; 10:9; 14:6). In other words, if I want to know with certainty my purpose on earth I need to consider the words of Jesus of Nazareth.

In a famous passage of Augustine's <u>Confessions</u> he stated: "You have made us for yourself, O Lord, and our heart is restless until it rests in you." One of the meditations (Pensees) attributed to Blaise Pascal was: "There is a God-shaped vacuum in the heart of every person, and it can never be filled by any created thing. It can only be filled by God, made known through Jesus Christ."

"What about the heathen?" is a question often asked by those who find it hard to believe that faith in Jesus is the only way to obtain eternal life. But everyone who is born again knows that no other name has been given by which we are to be saved (Acts 4:12). Jesus spoke about the narrow gate in the context of pretenders who would propose alternative paths to God (Matthew 7:13-23).

To talk about idol worship in the 21st century seems out of place. However it is prophesied that some time in the future a third of the world's population will be killed in a cataclysmic event. That will nevertheless not bring an end to the worship of idols made of gold, silver, bronze, stone and wood (Revelation 9:18,20). But at the moment idols are more likely to be made of silicon and tantalum, the raw materials needed in the manufacture of electronic devices.

Our culture is awash in images of celebrities who are idol worshipped by their fans. The famous are often aware of having a stage personality (persona) different from what they regard as their authentic self. To some extent this phenomenon is present in all of us. We don't display all our character traits to the world. It is possible for me to idolise my own image like Narcissus in the Greek legend.

In totalitarian societies personality cults are the order of the day. Pictures of the leader are on display and subjects of the regime are required to treat them with respect. This will ultimately find its most extreme expression in worship of the "beast" (Revelation 13:4, 8).

Paul equated greed with idolatry (Ephesians 5:5). When he wrote this letter John may have been thinking of Judas who was motivated by money (John 12:6). Paul warned that the desire to be rich is a snare (1 Timothy 6:9). Jesus spoke of money as the other "master" competing for our devotion (Luke 16:13). He warned against its lure again and again (Luke 6:24; 12:20-21; 16:9).

Printed in Great Britain
by Amazon

77806603R00047